CW01500832

# THE GREAT DISORDER

**An American Manifesto for a New World Order**

## ZACK SPRATLING

# THE
# GREAT
# DISORDER

*For my Dear, Amanda*

# Contents

# Preface

This is a book for all Americans. It is also a book for anyone looking to make sense of the recent chaos and significant shifts in America's relationship with the world. As a result, and considering the stakes at play for Americans and global order as a whole, this book is both diagnostic and prescriptive. Yet, it has also been published for ease of reading and written to be intentionally brief – a pocket guide for readers to come back to time and again to leverage its main ideas to drive principled change.

As you read, you will find that I often reference the past and look ahead to the future, but *The Great Disorder* was written for this very moment in geopolitical history.

Its primary goals are to decipher the driving forces of the current American presidential administration, provide an unbiased perspective on both the good and bad, and map out a new way forward for a world order driven by three foundational principles rooted in American values.

Throughout the book, you may find yourself agreeing with some points and disagreeing with others. I encourage you to take this as a cue for further discussion, not a final verdict to end it.

Lastly, the *Appendix* provides a light but foundational take on American interests and values – referred to throughout the main text.

These concepts may not come as a surprise to many Americans, but are worthy of review by all.

To this point, my single ask of you is to share these ideas with your friends, family, community – and in the case of *The American Values Meal* described in the *Appendix* – even a child in your life.

Although I have provided the beginnings of a recommended path forward, *The Great Disorder* is not intended to be a final solution, but rather an inspiration: an American manifesto to turn global chaos into a new, principled world order.

# Introduction

Has the world felt chaotic recently? If so, it might be because no one has told you the new rules. To introduce you to these, let's start by taking a walk in the jungle.

What's the first thing that comes to mind when you enter?

If you've watched *The Jungle Book,* maybe it's waterfalls, lush vegetation, and even a dancing bear or two. But here's the thing about the jungle

– it's lovely… until it isn't. That bear is cuddly and dancing one moment, then mauling your friend to steal his last stick of beef jerky, the next.

But hey, it's the *law of the jungle: the strong do what they can, and the weak suffer what they must*. This is a law that is well understood in the jungle, and no one knows it better than its king.

In America, the law of the jungle stands in stark contrast to the rule of law we value. Yet, it is currently the driving force defining American leadership's newly established *rules of the game*.

# The New Rules

Every game has a reset button, and the game of global politics is no different. However, it's usually wars between *great powers* that force a reset, such as the two world wars of the 20th century. Not this time. For the first time in over 80 years, a great power – the United States – is unilaterally pressing the reset button and shaking up the global order the world has known since the end of World War II.

Unlike historical precedents, the most unique characteristic of this situation is that it was the U.S. that *established* the current order, sits at the top of it, and yet is the one choosing to flip over the board and establish new rules – a strategy typically reserved for a losing player, not the leader.

Although these new rules may appear to be elusive and lacking strategic rationale, based on observation of the current Trump administration's actions alone, there *are* three general rules that we can extract from this new game – a game I call, *The Great Disorder*.

# Rule #1: Might Makes Right

The amount of global power the United States has accumulated since its founding, relative to the rest of the world, is unprecedented. Over many decades, American power developed slowly, then suddenly, when the trend accelerated dramatically at two inflection points in recent history: the end of World War II (WWII) and the Cold War.

Out of the ashes of WWII in 1945, two superpowers emerged – the U.S. and the Soviet Union – but by the time the Soviet Union took its last breath and the Cold War ended in 1991, only the U.S. remained.

Looking back at the first inflection point at the end of WWII, Europe and Asia were devastated, staring down a long road to recovery, and still attempting to settle many border disputes as a result of the fallout of the war and the weakening grip of empires of the past. Even the Soviets, quickly flipping from American ally in the war to geopolitical rival afterwards, had a significant rebuilding process ahead of them, including recovering from the death of well over 20 million people in the war – the largest amount of any country.

In contrast to the rest of the world powers, due to the sacrifices of the Greatest Generation, America was in a position where it dominated a comparatively peaceful western hemisphere. And, in the eastern hemisphere, had established military forces on both ends of the Eurasian supercontinent as a result of achieving victory with the Allies in both western Europe and east Asia.

America also emerged from the war with a thriving economy and industrial base at home, as well as a monopoly (if only for a few years) on the most powerful weapon the world had ever seen – the atomic bomb.

At this moment in history, if America had chosen a 'might makes right' approach, several things *could* have happened: territorial domination and exploitation of a valuable but severely weakened western Europe, subjugation and plundering of European colonies denying their forthcoming achievement of national sovereignty, the annexation of Japan as the '48th state,' etc.

The possibilities were endless, and if taken, all these actions *could* have been backstopped by the "fire and fury" of nuclear annihilation of anyone that resisted American might.

You get the point. Whether these actions would have been moral or wise is beside the point of appreciating the implications of *Rule #1*. You will likely judge them as immoral today, but remember that the morality of 'might makes right' is not defined by principles or national values, it is defined by ability; might; raw power.

Of course, this is not the path America chose. Which is not to say that the U.S. did not grow its power – it absolutely did – but it would require a willing blindness to the ruthless history of global politics and a lack of imagination to conclude that the power that was gained by America at the time was the limit of what was achievable with less constrained global ambition.

America made a *strategic* choice. And with the benefit of hindsight, it is now clear that it was the right one, ushering in an American, as well as global, economic, industrial, and technological renaissance period. Americans of 1945 had the foresight and wisdom to lean into our *north star*, and nobly lead the world with American values, while continuing to vigorously defend American interests.

After the war, the U.S. established economic and security *interdependencies* between the nations of the world to create shared interests that made a future world war unattractive to all involved. America also invested in the development and future prosperity of friend (Britain, France, etc.) and foe (Germany, Japan, etc.) alike.

Would Americans make that same choice today? I believe we would – it's in our DNA. But, current trends are not in favor of that choice. As satisfying as it may be to flex our geopolitical muscle on the global stage, flexing to inflict pain does not serendipitously solve ours. To be sure, there are nagging imbalances between the U.S. and the world that we need to address, such as trade that is not mutually beneficial or that is even domestically destructive, and a global military that is overextended and taken for granted by allies.

Moreover, we've got genuine, substantial problems to solve at home as well: industrial dependencies on adversaries, population growth that has become dependent on illegal immigration due to an overly difficult legal immigration process coupled with declining birth rates domestically, and younger generations that have (not completely without reason) become apathetic towards the American identity and dream.

Yet, the messier the outside world becomes, the harder it will be to solve these problems at home. And in a world of 'might makes right' where national borders are no longer respected, foundational institutions are broken and not rebuilt stronger, and the voices of the majority are silenced by the minority in power, things will get messier. The world has seen that movie before, and it is not an easy one to turn off.

As, when it comes to 'might makes right' for ambitious dictators of the world, as savvy and independent as they may be running the highest office in their land, the approach they are likely to take in this new world of the past is actually quite elementary – monkey see, monkey do.

## Rule #2: Friends with No Benefits

As the American colonies were signing the Declaration of Independence with one hand and giving Britain's King George III the one-finger salute with the other, America was already receiving covert support from France. The Founders secured America's *first* formal alliance with the Kingdom of France less than two years after the Declaration was signed, in 1778.

Even in those early days of the nation, this was a *mutually beneficial* relationship: America received troops, arms, and money from France, while the French saw a strategic opportunity to weaken its archrival in Europe by tying the British down in a protracted conflict with the Americans.

Since then, America has pursued alliances off-and-on, but like many things, our alliance network accelerated in the aftermath of WWII. This was especially useful throughout the Cold War, as we battled the Soviets for global influence. Each superpower used both attraction and coercion of potential allies to best the other in the cutthroat 40+ year competition.

But, the Soviets struggled, long-term, to consistently attract other powerful nations of the world and even its immediate neighbors to its communist style of governance. Alternatively, the U.S. was much more successful building a broad and durable ally network by attracting nations to American values, culture, and increasingly unmatched economic and military power.

These alliances have generally been considered a national asset, with the key assumption being that they are relationships of *mutual benefit*. Intuitively, this seems obvious, but as America's alliances grew wider throughout the Cold War and after, American leadership became less and less effective at articulating the value of these relationships to everyday Americans. Leadership became more interested in maintaining the status quo for the sake of continuity, rather than regularly assessing the costs and benefits of these alliances to the American people.

Where significant benefits did exist, leaders did not effectively explain these in a way the majority of Americans could identify with, and candidly, care enough to preserve.

One of those Americans happened to be Donald Trump. Beginning in the first Trump administration in 2017 and even before, the President's nature of drawing attention to issues with over-the-top statements laid bare some of the imbalances and contradictions in America's international relationships. Yet, what we should do about it was less clear.

For example, regarding our North Atlantic Treaty Organization (NATO) allies and defense spending, every U.S. president since Eisenhower in the 1950s has asked Europe to spend more on its defense, but this has, until very recently, not been effective.

As another example, considering the Middle East as a whole, for decades U.S. presidents have attempted to disengage from conflicts in the region, but each inevitably experiences a crisis that sucks America back in.

The story has been similar for our relationships with adversaries. Every president since the fall of the Soviet Union has attempted to create better relations between the U.S./NATO and Russia, only to fall short or even make existing tensions even worse. And, regarding global trade, it is beyond an open secret and long common knowledge that China's leadership has abused the international trading system America invited them into, to their advantage, for decades (e.g., currency manipulation, forced intellectual property transfer and theft, and more).

So clearly, America's approach to international relations was ready for disruption and new thinking. Yet, treating our friends (i.e., allies and partners) the same, if not worse, as our adversaries is not likely the new thinking most Americans expected. The closer the friend the tougher the treatment: Canada we threaten to make a state; Mexico we threaten to invade; and Denmark – a reliable NATO ally – we threaten to take their territory of Greenland.

All of this, while at the same time we go out of our way to stroke the ego of Russia's leader and praise the intellect of China's. There is something to be said for keeping your friends close and your enemies closer, but *respect* for an adversary should not be easily confused with *admiration*.

To be sure, there is no shortage of legitimate issues with our friends that need persistent attention. But, even if some friends require a tough love approach, and some adversaries require a soothing finesse, there is a fundamental truth at the root of these relationships that needs to be remembered. In the end, friends want each other to succeed, while adversaries want each other to fail.

While we can respect our adversaries' abilities, and even work to turn them into friends over time (e.g., Germany and Japan after WWII), we ignore this fundamental truth at our own risk. Alternatively, by remembering it, we remind ourselves that despite the difficulties, the values and interests that we share with our friends are a long-term benefit worth preserving.

Ultimately, even if our current public demands to our friends are part of a negotiating tactic and not serious statements, some things will be difficult for the world to unhear and unsee. We should remain a tough negotiator, but cast aside the unproductive public humiliation of friends, and turn up the heat (but not disrespect) publicly on adversaries.

Irrespective of American power, there should be no doubt that if the world evolves further under *Rule #1: Might Makes Right*, friends are only going to increase in value. Although not immediately on the horizon, future conflict is inevitable, and the only thing worse than fighting with friends is fighting without them.

# Rule #3: It's All About the Benjamins Baby

This rule speaks for itself. In *The Great Disorder*, there is no problem that can't be solved by making an economic deal. Whether it's an adversary or one of our oldest allies, every relationship is increasingly defined first and foremost by its immediate economic value to the United States. One of the most recent and controversial examples of this approach is what President Trump has called "the most beautiful word in the dictionary" – tariffs.

Since trade and tariffs are all the rage these days, yet notoriously complex, I'm going to highlight this topic specifically for *Rule #3*, making sense of the chaos and focusing on what matters to everyday Americans.

## Trade & Tariffs

Before we attempt to get a handle on what is going on with tariffs, we first need to understand the (very) basics of global trade. For the purposes of following current political discussions, here's what you need to know.

In our economy, we create both *goods* (e.g., furniture, energy, food, airplanes, etc.) and *services* (e.g., travel, education, financial and technology services, etc.). When the U.S. provides a good or service to another country, this is called an *export*; when another country provides it to the U.S., this is called an *import*. When we export more than we import, this is called a *trade surplus*; and, when we import more than we export, it's called a *trade deficit*.

Further, trade surpluses and deficits are most notably tracked at an overall level (e.g., the U.S.

with the rest of the world), or, between single nations in what's called *bilateral trade* (e.g., the U.S. with China). Lastly, whether overall or bilaterally, trade can be tracked separately for goods, separately for services, or as a combined total.

It can get much more detailed and complicated than this, but you've now got the basics you need as an informed American able to understand the political debates that impact your wallet and community. If you need to rewind, and run this last paragraph back on half speed, do so, your future self will thank you.

What you have been hearing most in the news regarding trade is that America has a large trade deficit with the world. This is true for overall trade, and for goods specifically. This is *not* true for services.

Without causing your eyes to glaze over like a freshly made donut, here's a few *ballpark* figures for you to keep in your back pocket to impress family and friends: the U.S. exports around $3 trillion, and imports around $4 trillion of goods and services (i.e., we have an overall trade deficit). Within those numbers, goods make up about $2 trillion of our exports and $3 trillion of our imports (i.e., we have a trade deficit in *goods* specifically).

If you're following the money so far, you'll realize that our global trade in *services* is actually fairly balanced – around $1 trillion both exported and imported – and due to the ballpark figures I've provided, more precisely, services exports actually *exceed* imports by a couple hundred billion dollars (i.e., we actually have a trade *surplus* in services). For whatever reason, the Trump administration's comments and numbers on trade provided to the public have mainly focused on goods, not services trade. But what I've just provided is the full picture at the highest level.

Here are a few other remarks you may have heard from politicians regarding U.S. trade.

- ♦ 'Our largest trading partners are now the European Union (EU), Mexico, and Canada, not China' – this is true, although China is still significant.
- ♦ 'We have large trade *deficits* with China, the EU, Mexico, and Vietnam' – this is true, with the deficit with China being by far the largest, but all greater than $100 billion each.
- ♦ 'The world economy is more reliant on exporting to the U.S. than the U.S. is reliant on exporting to the world' – this is generally a true statement, and does

provide the U.S. with leverage in current trade negotiations.

♦ 'The U.S. is the largest *services* exporter in the world' – you may not have heard this one yet, but it is also true, and around $1 trillion as previously mentioned (nearly double that of the second ranked United Kingdom).

Lastly, and most importantly, you may have heard that 'trade deficits are bad' – this is *not* true in all cases. And this point is key. Is a persistent, multi-decade, 100s of billions of dollars and growing trade deficit with our primary global adversary (China), bad? Absolutely. However, on the other end of the trade spectrum, if a small island nation sends us tons of coffee that we can't grow here, but is a relatively poor country and can't afford to buy a bunch of U.S. products, is that bilateral trade deficit a 'bad' situation? No, not unless you have an ungodly disdain for good coffee.

Okay, so now you're a trade expert. But, what do *tariffs* have to do with trade? Tariffs are an additional amount – it's reasonable to call it a 'government tax' – added to the cost of goods and/or services imported to the U.S. (or whichever country is imposing the tariff).

For example, Bob from Iowa used to buy a chair that is made in China on Amazon for $125 – and, let's say Amazon originally purchased the chair from a Chinese manufacturer for $100. The U.S. then decides to impose a 50% tariff on everything Americans buy from China. Amazon will now need to pay $150 for the same chair – the original $100 to the Chinese manufacturer, and an *additional* $50 that will be the tariff amount paid directly to the U.S. government. Meanwhile, Bob back in Iowa *could* now pay $175 for his chair – the original price of $125, *plus* the $50 tariff amount that Amazon *may* pass through to Bob by raising the price of the chair.

Pause here and chew a bit if math makes you nauseous. This is a crucial point to digest to understand what all these politicians and talking heads are saying about tariffs.

Now, notice the emphasis I put on what Bob *could* pay, and what Amazon *may* do. The following explanation is one of a handful of uncertainties as to why two different people – say a Republican and Democratic politician – can have the same information, assume opposite outcomes to fit their political agenda, and claim vastly different impacts on the American people. In our example, it is highly unlikely that Bob will continue to pay the original *$125* for his chair – but it is also unlikely that he will pay *$175*.

The reason, is because *both* Amazon and the Chinese manufacturer will likely work to lower their price in order to keep selling chairs. However, there are limits to how low they can go, and if either can't make a profit selling the chair, they won't sell it. In the end, all we can say with *confidence* is that Bob is very likely going to pay more for his chair – as long as it's made in China, and as long as the U.S. imposes tariffs on Chinese made chairs. Lastly, what we can say with *certainty* is that the U.S. government *will* be paid a 50% tariff amount for each of these chairs imported into the U.S.

Okay, now take a deep breath... then apply this scenario to all $3 trillion of goods we import into the U.S. The current tariff rates and target countries can change with the next social media post, but this situation is why many people conclude that Americans will *likely pay more* for foreign products as a result of the current trade war – in other words, *inflation*. But just *how much* inflation is unclear.

Further, this is why even President Trump has acknowledged that there will be "some pain" in the *short-term*. That pain he's referring to is primarily inflation, and even the potential for some foreign goods to disappear from American storefronts altogether. Yet, why is the President emphasizing the *short-term*?

The reason the short-term is emphasized by the Trump administration is due to their ultimate goal for using tariffs. Their goal as explained by them typically goes like this: in the short-term, tariffs will raise money that the government can then use to reduce the national debt and enable tax cuts for Americans, while in the long-term, tariffs will have the effect of forcing companies to make the goods they sell to Americans, in America, creating American jobs, and revitalizing American manufacturing as a result.

The problem with this goal according to opponents of tariffs, namely many businesses and mainstream economists, is typically summarized like this: tariffs make global trade inefficient by disincentivizing countries from focusing on making *what they make best*; tariffs artificially raise prices for Americans, while also raising input costs for American businesses and making their end products more expensive to sell; and lastly, tariffs slow economic growth overall.

So, who's right? The reality is that there is truth in both perspectives, but which side you agree with will come down to what you prioritize, or in other words, what matters to you most. As you consider that, here are a few key questions to ask yourself.

Should we prioritize lower prices for American consumers or more jobs for American workers? In some cases, we may be able to achieve both, but in many cases – due to the fact that on average foreign factory workers are paid 60% less than American factory workers – these two goals are incompatible. American labor is not cheap. That being said, *prices* are irrelevant if people do not have *jobs*.

So, if we *do* prioritize jobs, which jobs should we prioritize? Are all jobs created equally? Is our ability to grow our own food, generate energy, and make weapons domestically, as important as making our own dining chairs and dolls? This is not to say we cannot make chairs and dolls in America, but do we need to make *all* of them – what and how do we prioritize?

Further, ask yourself, prices and jobs aside, should we generally prioritize our capability to "make things" in America? And, should we do so even if those things could be made cheaper elsewhere?

These are all important, legitimate questions in the tariff debate that get to the heart of the matter, which is that *tradeoffs* are a reality in the decisions that we make, and the consequences of those decisions have real world impacts – some good, some bad, and some unknown at the time.

As we look ahead towards solutions in the final section of this book – *A Strategy for The New Order* – I'll address some of the tradeoffs and provide my net perspective on trade and tariffs.

Trade is one notable example of *Rule #3* in *The Great Disorder*, but it is by no means the only one. Americans know that there is more to a relationship than money, but does our current leadership? America has always been the land of the go-getter, but just as most Americans put guardrails on what they are willing to sacrifice to make a buck, so too should our nation.

As we look back at *The New Rules*, it starts to become clear that playing by these could have, many, unintended consequences – for the world, but also for America.

# A Road Unknown

So now you know the rules of *The Great Disorder* – Might Makes Right, Friends with No Benefits, and It's All About the Benjamins Baby – but a key question remains: what will the outcome of this new game be?

On this road unknown, Americans, and even the world, have to wonder – what will it look like on the other side? Of course, when the driver can change his mind at any moment based on gut feelings, no one – not even the driver – can know for sure. However, with an understanding of: the new rules of the game, America's relationship with the world, and historical precedents, we can begin to see a few possible outcomes.

Before we discuss these outcomes, and for the benefit of all sane citizens of the world, I'm going to first address the driver of this new journey – or perhaps, rollercoaster – that we're all on. Regardless of political affiliation, we should all come to grips with a few realities.

President Trump is not Adolf Hitler. President Trump is also not Jesus Christ Superstar. He is a father, husband, and the (very) powerful President of the United States. Yet, he is also just a man, and like any man – no matter his achievements – is unworthy of idolatry. He is the definition of polarizing, with a legion of followers as large as his legion of opposers. He has a *huuuge* ego with an endless need for stroking and ripe for manipulation by the strategically astute leaders of the world. But, he is also a relentless hustler, courageous, and unapologetically patriotic. He is not bad, and he is not good – he is both.

Further, given that he earned the right to hold the office of the President of the United States (POTUS) twice over, his ideas should be taken seriously and with respect. Yet, it is with respect that I say, some of his ideas are complete garbage and they should be called out as such (e.g., annexing Canada as the 51$^{st}$ state against Canadians' will, forcefully exiling Palestinians to make Gaza a "Riviera of the Middle East", and blatantly ignoring the benefits of *legal* immigration to the U.S.).

It's worth mentioning that we all have really bad ideas at times, but the difference for most of us is that we test them out in private, personal settings before we unleash them on the world. The worst ones are taken out back, shot, and never see the light of day.

However, the President's unfiltered style is one in which he tests his ideas out on the world in real time. In his position of POTUS, he is clearly playing with fire, but words are not actions, and like it or not, this is the President's method of operating.

Moreover, in contrast to those less than stellar ideas, others the President has are refreshingly bold, honest, and in the best interests of the American people (e.g., secure national borders, the Abraham Accords, a consistent bias towards peace over war, and the reprioritization of American industry).

Americans should not hide from these facts about the President in order to unquestioningly turn our decision making over to our favorite conservative or progressive channel. I find it tortuously frustrating to watch our "leaders" do this while tucking their tails and obediently sitting themselves in their 'Republican' or 'Democrat' ideological boxes, never missing a note from their party song sheets.

Our leaders should be courageous enough to call it like it is, political consequences be damned. But unfortunately, it has become as if Congress is where courage and honor go to die. This should not, and does not, have to be the case.

Americans deserve better, and I will discuss what that 'better' looks like as we discuss solutions in the final section. With that said, let's hop back on our rollercoaster for a moment: where could President Trump and his administration be taking us? I'm going to start with some of the undesirable outcomes, as, I'll acknowledge some of the better ones when we discuss a path forward. The following are *three* overarching challenges that I expect to emerge along the current road we are on – you could call them warnings, to the wise.

# Challenge #1: More Instability

With our new rules in place, we can fully expect a more fractured, unstable global security and economic environment. This means that as the world becomes less integrated, and relationships fray, it will increasingly become a world of 'us versus them.' Not just from an American perspective, but from the perspective of each individual nation of the world.

Yet keep in mind, as I discussed above, the major powers of the world, including the U.S., have already experimented with a go-it-alone approach and we got two devastating world wars out of it.

Think of it this way: when we eliminate the interdependencies that bind the world together (even as imperfect as they are), other nations of the world become 'those people over there.' And, as these feelings grow over time, it becomes easier and easier to dislike, hate, and eventually even go to war with 'those people.' We do not understand them and they do not understand us; the other side is not like us; the other side becomes less than. War becomes more likely.

This escalation in hate to war is not inevitable, but if you translate the 'us versus them' concept to your personal life and relationships, you will understand that conflict becomes increasingly more likely as the stakes get higher and disagreements arise.

While it is true that a reprioritization by American leadership of Americans' interests over global interests was sorely needed, we do not have to abandon the good with the bad.

As, when we begin to crack nearly 100-year-old global institutions and even 250-year-old American institutions with no plan for revitalization, we are asking for an earthquake of historic proportions – with consequences unknown.

# Challenge #2: Less Freedom

As we continue down the road we are on, it has become clear that autocrats and other leaders of the world not fairly elected by the people they govern, are getting more comfortable in this new world. It is also true that, with an increasing concentration of power in single leaders, disrespect for established term limits, and election meddling, democracies of the world look less stable.

However, to be clear, the fair election of a candidate one does not vote for is not a failure of democracy, it is, like it or not, a success. But nonetheless, the rise of supposed 'saviors' that believe they have a right to eternal power and speak for *everyone* in their nation on *every* issue, is increasing, and should make freedom-loving people very anxious.

Because of course, in your own country, even if you love the political savior of today, there is no guarantee that you will love the one of tomorrow.

As Americans, looking inwards at ourselves and out at the world that is taking shape under the new rules, we should not view words like 'democracy' and 'autocracy' merely as buzzwords. The first means you are free, heard, and have individual liberty, while the other means you are guaranteed none of those things.

Americans told Britain's king to kick rocks nearly 250 years ago, and I know we have no desire to return to being subject to the whims of hereditary kings of the past. We are still far from this, but if you think it's impossible that this could happen in America, then you have decided to ignore the long arch of history, with all its twists, turns, and occasional civilizational collapses.

But even as we retain our strong democratic traditions, as I'm confident we will, we have to be wary of a world where other autocratic nations grow increasingly powerful. Even if you love America so much you never plan to go outside of it, in a world of intercontinental ballistic missiles and increasingly sophisticated cyber and space warfare, no one or thing is out of reach of the long arm of chaos. We cannot fully wall ourselves off from threats.

Yet, if the world is not led by America, someone will eventually fill that gap. Perhaps it would be our ideological twin, but it looks more likely that it would be nothing of the sort – such as the autocratic and illiberal China or Russia – and their leadership has already shown that they will clearly not be content to stay in their small corner of the world.

# Challenge #3: Lost Influence

Considering these first two challenges, and understanding the new rules of the game, America should be prepared for a world where we have less of an ability to *influence* these outcomes. While American economic and military power are obvious forms of influence, American brand and diplomatic power is a more silent, yet very powerful, force globally. This provides significant advantages that cannot always be cashed in or profited from immediately, but they are there nonetheless.

America has always had isolationist tendencies, and if you pull up a map of the world, it quickly becomes apparent as to why. Yet, Americans still understand that having more influence is better than less. What we must also realize is that although we have accumulated significant national power over the centuries, as we squeeze the world tighter and tighter, with the goal of not just winning, but dominating every situation we find ourselves in – squeezing out every last penny and concession – we will inevitably decrease our brand and diplomatic power. This could ultimately negatively impact our economic power, and as a result, even military power.

This is not to say that we should be afraid to use power, but we should do so in a thoughtful way that *empowers* both us and our allies, *deters* our adversaries from crossing us, and when necessary, *dominates* our enemies.

As we continue down this road unknown, these are three challenges we must be prepared for without a course correction. Yet, despite the decisions already made, how favorable or not the outcome of *The Great Disorder* is to American prosperity is *still* dependent on choices yet to be made.

Therefore, to put the nation in the best position in these times of persistent uncertainty, what's unequivocally required from our leaders is an unbiased acknowledgement of the good ideas, a courageous rejection of the bad, and most critically, an actual *strategy* for American success.

# A Strategy for
# The New Order

The board has been flipped over, *The Great Disorder* has begun, and the new rules have been established. Regardless of which side of the political aisle you sit on, this much we should all be able to agree on. The question for Americans to ask now is not *where* we're going, but where *should* we go, and *how* do we get there.

The first question is the easiest to answer, yet the easiest to lose sight of and lose our way. The answer to where we *should* go, is driven by America's *north star.* Hear me out. Before you conclude that this book has devolved into a lullaby, consider this situation.

Whether you are someone who bows your head or someone who looks up into the dark abyss of space, most of us have, at some point, reflected deeply on questions such as: What is this life all about? And, what is my purpose here? Just as individuals deliberate these identity-defining questions, nations must do the same. And, just like individuals, if not answered by the nation and its leaders *explicitly*, the world will fill that void and define your path for you.

This is why it is essential that America stays true to our north star: *Leading with American Values & Defending American Interests.* This is more than a catchphrase or slogan, because it connects directly with the past that Americans hold dear as well as the future we desire. It is about freedom, rights, opportunity, prosperity and more. I discuss this specific topic in more detail in the *Appendix* at the end of this book, but for now, just know that *American values and interests* are the essence of our north star.

So, if that is what's guiding us, what does it look and feel like when it's put into action?

Thinking back to the three rules of *The Great Disorder* that we discussed, it becomes clear that this is *not* what it looks like. These rules are not sustainable for American security and prosperity. They are *disruptive*, and there is something to be said for the benefits and growth that can come from disrupting the old way of doing things – as, this is famously the ethos of America's most successful companies of this century. But, by definition, disruption is a temporary state of being, and this is particularly so for a nation.

So, looking ahead and thinking strategically about how the American experiment can, not just survive, but thrive in the years ahead of us, we have to reassess the *temporary rules* we've set and identify more *lasting principles* that are fit for the moment, aligned with our north star, and that reinforce America's foundation.

I propose three.

# Principle #1: Protect This House

As I have discussed before, America's role in global affairs for the better part of the past century has been "indispensable" to global security and prosperity (a few black eyes aside). This arrangement brought immense benefits to America, as well as to the world. Yet, one of the greatest delusions of American leadership over the past few decades was that the 'people of the world' (in the most generic sense) mattered just as much or even more than the 'people of America.'

While in the grand scheme of life, it is *absolutely true* that every person matters as much as the next, irrespective of where on Earth they reside, from the specific perspective of America's *elected* leaders, this is *absolutely not true*, and fundamentally *cannot* be true for a healthy nation.

Should this not be a truism for any nation's leaders? If America's leaders do not prioritize Americans, then who will? American leadership must prioritize Americans security and prosperity over all else. Period.

This is not to say that we should go scorched earth on the rest of the world. We should strive to lift the people of the world up as well, and we generally have for at least 80 years. Yet, we still must be mindful of history, and the potential for charismatic leaders to morph genuine patriotism into militaristic nationalism with a superiority complex. This can easily lead to the dehumanization of 'others' outside of a nation's borders, and ultimately even war. It is critical that we avoid this extreme.

Yet, to insinuate that one extreme or the other is necessary is to create a false choice. American leadership that is competent *and* empathetic should and can do both, while prioritizing appropriately.

American Presidents of the recent past have skewed more toward one extreme or the other, with President Trump's rhetoric skewing heavily towards rightly lifting up Americans, but unnecessarily disparaging the people of the world.

However, on the whole, if there is one of the three principles I'm proposing in which the Trump administration has made the most progress, it is this one.

There are two primary examples of this.

## Secure Borders

The first is securing the nation's borders. America's immigration policy has been asinine for awhile, but it has only gotten worse, peaking in its insanity in 2023. This is not political rhetoric. This is backed by common sense and official immigration data that is widely available. To that point, the new Trump administration has made significant progress on illegal migrant border crossings. This is a step in the right direction.

That being said, I have significant concerns about the rhetoric President Trump uses on this topic. It's more than words, because it has also shown its face in how we are treating *recent* immigrants, illegal *and* legal. I emphasize *recent*, because although it may sound cliché, we *are* in fact a nation mostly of immigrants. I fully believe that most Americans still appreciate this fact.

Which is why degrading immigrants (e.g., calling them rapists, terrorists, etc.) is not just silly, but also irresponsible. *Most likely*, the majority of illegal immigrants that have crossed the U.S. border recently are non-criminals, fleeing badly governed countries, and risking their life to make a better one – a story that would likely sound familiar to many Americans' ancestors.

Although the *American Dream* may feel dead at times, it is not dead to most Americans, and it is certainly not dead to the world.

Now, if we acknowledge this, we also must acknowledge that *some* illegal immigrants were likely career criminals or even terrorists. It would be irrational to conclude otherwise. Because, if you are an adversary of the United States, in a leadership position in a criminal cartel, military or intelligence agency, and *did not* send at least a few human assets across the border during the past few years of border chaos, you should lose your job. It was a golden opportunity for America's adversaries, taken or not.

From an American perspective, just one nefarious actor crossing the border illegally is one too many, but the reality is that we simply *do not know* who all came across, and that is unacceptable.

So here we are. We move forward by securing the border (check), changing our rhetoric, and finally fixing our legal immigration system. Assuming the cowardly lions in Congress rediscover their courage to govern, I'll leave the topic of our legal immigration process for another day, and lastly address the President's immigration rhetoric.

Mr. President, I recommend trying this one on for size:

"My fellow Americans, people of the world, the American border is now secure. America is a nation with a strong rule of law, but we are also a nation of immigrants. We welcome the people of the world to our beautiful country. Americans love the world, but we believe there is no better place on Earth than the United States of America.

If you come to our country legally, to paraphrase one of our nation's Founders – Benjamin Franklin – we will guarantee your right to pursue happiness, but you will have to catch it. Americans will support you in that pursuit.

Alternatively, if you come to our country illegally – and especially if you come with bad intentions – you will be met by the most capable border agents and most powerful military in the world.

You know, my detractors think I'm crazy – I'm not – but I wouldn't try me.

Do.not.come.illegally. ... Come here legally, come to America, and add your chapter to the greatest success story in the history of the world."

Something like this Mr. President, give or take, but please keep the name-calling and all caps to a minimum, sir.

## Global Trade

Moving on from immigration and wrapping up *Principle #1: Protect This House,* another example of this principle where the Trump administration has already made some progress is in global trade. To be clear, the specific *policies* around trade and tariffs recently have resembled a two-step shuffle of a bar drunk at closing time – one step this way, three the other, stop, start… where's he going next?, no one knows. In other words, very confusing and erratic. However, that does not mean that the *inspiration* for these new trade policies is entirely misguided.

When we discussed trade and tariffs at length earlier in this book, recall that we talked about the 'right' solution depending on what you choose to prioritize (e.g., prices, jobs, etc.). From a pure *market* perspective, you will almost always conclude that tariffs are bad, which has been the prevailing opinion in America for many decades – not too surprising for a highly capitalistic economy.

However, there is a fundamental problem with this conclusion for our current situation. Even if you ignore the significant trade barriers some nations have had in place for years – namely one of our largest trading partners, China – a pure market perspective on trade barriers and tariffs does not adequately consider *non-market* factors, such as the importance of making things domestically and the impact on communities left behind due to jobs moved overseas.

These issues are not new to American leadership, but they have only recently begun to address them. Left behind manufacturing communities is an issue that has been festering for 50+ years for a multiplicity of reasons, but it accelerated significantly when China entered the global trading system in 2001. Moreover, the importance of making things in America was only recently exposed to everyone as a significant vulnerability in 2020 due to COVID, even if some still remain unconvinced of the necessity of domestic manufacturing.

Despite this timeline, the first Trump administration was already bringing these issues to light back in 2016, and slowly began to make progress upon taking office. Yet, it was the Biden administration that accelerated this progress with Congressional legislation, such as the 2022 CHIPS Act. Now, President Trump is clearly positioning to make these issues a core theme of his second administration.

This being said, in order for any of the Trump administration's goals for tariffs to even have the *potential* to be achieved – national debt reduction, tax cuts, and domestic reindustrialization and job creation – tariffs will need to be sustained for *years*, especially for this last goal. Yet, a constantly changing tariff policy creates significant uncertainty for businesses, inhibiting them from having the confidence to take on the multi-year, multi-million or even billion-dollar investment projects required to build out new factories and businesses in the U.S. (i.e., create jobs and reindustrialize). Businesses need some level of policy predictability to make long-term investments like these.

If U.S. tariffs ultimately settle lower, say at 10%, this could be a sustainable level that American businesses and consumers adapt to. But for higher tariffs (e.g., 145% on China), it is all but certain that there will not be enough political will in Washington to withstand the discontent among American businesses and voters if costs increase and inflation rises. Only a few days into the initial tariff announcement on "liberation day," we already saw cracks in a durable tariff policy (e.g., 90-day pause on reciprocal tariffs, exclusion of electronic products from the higher rate tariffs on China, and more).

Expect these rollbacks to continue as voices of discontent grow louder, as setting extraordinarily high tariff rates on large trading partners is like playing with economic fire. Further, we should realize that tariffs are only one of many tools in our trade toolbox, and it should rarely, if ever, be our first choice. We should consider other tools as well, such as providing U.S. investment incentives, negotiating to reduce foreign trade barriers, providing priority access to strategic goods such as defense equipment, and more.

Considering everything we have discussed on trade and tariffs, and with *Principle #1: Protect This House* in mind, this is where I land on trade.

Global trade is a net positive for America – it increases business competition, lowers prices for Americans, and provides us with an unprecedented global catalog of goods and services to choose from, from the everyday essentials to luxury items. Trade also provides more markets for American businesses, enabling higher growth for those companies and the U.S. economy on the whole. Yet, American leadership must ensure that our trade relationships benefit not only large multinational corporations, but also American small businesses, while simultaneously improving the standard of living of everyday Americans.

If these benefits are not widely dispersed across all Americans; if trade relationships are grossly imbalanced; if America is overly exposed to trade with adversaries; or, if the country is losing our capability to produce critical goods (e.g., food, energy, semiconductors, steel, etc.) – America's leaders must act.

If this requires short-term disruption, for long-term gain, then this is the right choice for the nation. Yet, *how* we act matters. There is no guarantee that our actions will improve the situation, especially if they are haphazard, unfirm, and alienate allies.

Other countries *will* respond and we do not hold all the cards, but we should negotiate from a position of strength, with the goal of *mutually beneficial* trade, and knowing that the heft and dynamism of the American economy provide us with enormous leverage in protecting our house.

# Principle #2: Appreciate the Value of Relationships

We need to appreciate and *cherish* the value of our relationships. But we also need to appreciate and *increase* the value of our relationships. Are you picking up what I'm putting down?

Realize the value of good relationships, and improve the value of bad ones. Of course, there is typically a third option – exit the relationship – but this is rarely a realistic choice in geopolitics, especially for a global superpower like the United States.

This principle is particularly significant given that two of the three rules in *The Great Disorder* directly contradict it – *Rule #2: Friends with No Benefits*, and, *Rule #3: It's All About the Benjamins Baby.* In other words, the Trump administration has performed poorly on this principle.

Of course, the only thing predictable about the President is that he is unpredictable, so who knows what tomorrow will bring. And there *have* been bright spots – relations with the United Kingdom (UK) are healthy and improving; the President has always had a good relationship with India and our partners in the Middle East; and his attempt to improve relations with Russia is not a bad thing on its face, even as futile of an effort as it may be with their current leadership in charge.

However, the Trump administration's general approach to our international relationships has been, truly, perplexing. I find it difficult to believe that the President genuinely does not understand that there is more to a relationship than its immediate economic value. But if so, it is not obvious from his behavior. We all know he places a high premium on loyalty… so there is at least that.

But of course, there are many more sources of value in a relationship. Americans experience this everyday with our personal and professional relationships, and the similarity to nations is useful. Trust, respect, honesty, and a sense of mutual benefit, to list a few characteristics where each side receives value. And for nations specifically, there is national defense and intelligence support, diplomatic support, and in the U.S.' specific case, an acceptance and reverence for America's unique role as the leader of the free world.

If you think some of these sound fuzzy, I get it. But make no mistake, we've realized a lot of value in these areas with our allies and partners over the years. *Soft power* is real, and America has a lot – if we can keep it.

On the more obvious, harder side of the power ledger, the value to the U.S. that allies and partners provide through national defense and intelligence support *is* something I think is generally understood by the Trump administration.

However, we should continue to lean into this more, as I believe the President has a tendency to over rely on the fact that we have the most powerful military in the world. This may be true, but doing everything alone is costly, inefficient, and increasingly difficult for the U.S. to manage globally – recall what I said earlier about the only thing worse than fighting with friends…

## Friendly Relationships

With that broader view of the value of international relationships in mind, America must identify a shortlist of friendly relationships to prioritize, considering the state of global politics, among other things. There can always be more countries added to this list, but I'm going to focus here on the top priorities only.

## Canada & Mexico

We have to begin in our own back yard, with our neighbors – Canada and Mexico. In the past, I may not have even mentioned healthy relations with Canada and Mexico, as it was such a given, but clearly it needs to be reemphasized.

There are obvious reasons why we should have good relationships with these countries, such as our thousands of miles of shared land borders, population and cultural integration, shared democratic values, and significant economic integration. But, there is a broader, more strategic reason for good relations that may be less obvious to everyday Americans.

This is that the combination of our natural geography, energy independence, natural resources, and manufacturing and supply chain potential, creates the *ability* for North America to become a heavily self-reliant continent, *if necessary*.

I am not advocating that the U.S. fully embrace this scenario, but it is an advantageous position to be in and a possibility to consider, particularly if the likelihood of global instability continues to increase, as we discussed earlier in this book.

## Asia Pacific

Despite that potential isolationist scenario, that is not the world we live in today, and as such, our second relationship priority is on the other side of the world – our allies and partners in the Asia Pacific region. These nations are most prominently Japan, Australia, South Korea, India, and the Philippines, but there are more.

Not only does America have significant economic interests in this region of the world – just look at the 'Made in Country X' tag on many items in your house to see this first hand – but we have had a military presence in this region for well over a century, with a significant increase after World War II.

These economic and military interests, combined with the fact that our most capable global adversary – China – is in the region, makes our relationships in the Asia Pacific region highly valuable across many dimensions. Further, if our competition with China were unfortunately ever to escalate to conflict, our combined might in the region allows America to *defend forward* – or in other words, address conflicts far away from the homeland – a strategy the American military leverages across the world.

## Europe

Our third and final existing relationship priority is Europe. This is a continent obviously, not a single country, but due to the cohesion provided by the European Union (EU) and the overlap with the NATO military alliance with the U.S., it is best to first consider Europe as a bloc. However, it is the United Kingdom on Europe's periphery, France, and Germany that are the major powers with the most influence in the region.

The value of this relationship to America is deep and broad: the EU (taken as a bloc) is America's largest trading partner, American and European institutions and values have shared histories and a high degree of alignment to this day, and many Americans trace their ancestry back to European nations.

Further, the American military and defense industry's connectivity to European militaries primarily via the NATO alliance will become increasingly important – to Europe, as America requires it to do more to defend itself, and to America, as we prioritize the Asia Pacific region and may look to Europe to assist with the stability of regions the U.S. has historically secured (e.g., Middle Eastern shipping lanes).

## Adversarial Relationships

Pivoting to America's more adversarial relationships, our priority shifts to two nations with the greatest capabilities, and will, to negatively impact American security and prosperity – Russia and China.

## Russia

Remember that 40+ year Cold War with the Soviet Union we briefly discussed earlier? Not only was Russia the primary successor to the Soviets, many Soviet leaders continued on to lead the Russian state.

In fact, Russia's multi-decade leader, or, dictator – Vladimir Putin – was a deputy mayor of one of the Soviet Union's largest cities and an officer in the Soviet's infamous intelligence agency, the KGB. He has also called the fall of the Soviet

Union "the greatest geopolitical catastrophe of the century."

This is the starting point context of the U.S.-Russia relationship that one has to keep in mind when asking the innocent question, "why can't we just be friends with Russia?" Of course, as the two most heavily nuclear armed countries in the world, this would be great, and *should* continue to be a goal.

However, we cannot become blind to the current facts and ignorant of the past. As long as Putin remains in charge, true peace between the U.S. and Russia will remain incredibly difficult, if not impossible. Yet, this is *more* of a reason for us to value this relationship, not less.

Putin is manipulative and ruthless, but he is also strategic and much more reasonable than he is often portrayed. He has a particular mode of operation and a personal dictionary that does not contain words like "please" and 'freedom.' The language he understands is *force*, both verbal and physical. So. We tell him what we want, and if necessary, we show him. It's that simple.

Yet ultimately, we *do* need to keep working with the Russians to maintain global stability; we should genuinely appreciate the rich history of Russian culture and scientific achievements; and we need to respect, but not glorify, Putin as a leader of the Russian people.

The value of this relationship to the U.S. is straightforward at this moment in history – deter conflict and avoid all-out war.

**China**

Unlike our relationship with Russia, America's current relationship with China is much more complex. They are one of our largest trading partners, manufacture a significant amount of our goods (nearly a third of the world's), and the second largest foreign holder of American debt. They also have the world's second largest population, the second largest economy, and rapidly growing military power.

These facts alone do not make America's relationship with China adversarial. However, what *does* is an unelected single-party state with a leader – Xi Jinping – that has all but become a dictator in his own right, and who has a vision for the world that is made in the Chinese Communist Party's (CCP) image.

It is a vision which is fundamentally incompatible with the interests and values Americans hold dear. This vision, exemplified by Xi's decade-plus rule, is one that does not respect individual rights, personal freedom in the broadest sense, or democratic principles – which in its simplest conception is the ability for the people to have *some* say in who rules them.

Further, the more assertive and militaristic China becomes globally, as we have seen – particularly as it is against American allies and interests – the more likely conflict between the U.S. and China becomes. Yet, this is not a scenario anyone sane wants.

Therefore, like America's relationship with Russia, the desire to avoid conflict is *more* of a reason for us to value the Chinese relationship, not less. America and China together make up over a third of the world economy, so, for the sake of an ounce of global security and prosperity alone, we *must* manage our competition responsibly.

We should be committed to maintaining a peaceful coexistence, but actively resistant to becoming dependent on an adversary for, frankly, anything; we should respond unambiguously and with commanding dominance when China's military or intelligence operations cross the line; yet, we should also acknowledge China's enduring history and appreciate the Chinese people's incredible achievements and dynamism; and, we should remind Xi and the CCP that the Chinese people will continue on long after they are gone, so if they want to compete, that's fine, America is ready – but they should be prepared to lose.

Among many other reasons, but in no small part due to the nature of our adversarial relationships with Russia and China, it is clear that we need friends across the globe moving forward – more so now than in a long time.

America is a uniquely powerful nation, but our power *relative* to other nations is not what it was 30 years ago. We have to play smarter, and think more strategically. Doing this and retaining one of the U.S.' greatest assets – our friendships – keeps the global competitive advantage in America's favor and ensures American prosperity endures.

# Principle #3: Speak Softly and Carry a Big Stick

This phrase was popularized over a century ago by U.S. President Theodore "Teddy" Roosevelt, but the principle is timeless. It is a relevant concept for everyday Americans, but it's an especially potent principle for nations and their leaders.

Nation's leaders' words and actions often have real world impacts on global security and stability. The President of the United States uniquely wields this power with an unmatched ability to shake financial markets, strike fear (or joy) in heads of state, and even start and stop wars.

The Trump administration, and the President especially, leave a lot to be desired when it comes to this principle. President Trump's obsession with bravado and public shaming drives his opponents crazy and embarrasses moderates, but even his most passionate supporters acknowledge that it is a bit much.

But here's the thing: sounding tough does not make you tough. America, and by extension American leadership as its representative, happen to be both right now. But, our toughness is not *because* of our talk. Our talk is rather an unbecoming side effect of our *true* toughness as a nation.

The irony in the President's incessant behavior is that he *does* have toughness in his bones. Thin skin in places, yes, but there's toughness on the interior. Even if you're in the "never Trumper" or "not my president" camp, you cannot honestly watch his immediate response to an attempted assassination, and witness his ability to emerge as President for a second time after a barrage of legal jiu jitsu, and conclude President Trump is not a fighter.

As a recent alternate example, I don't think you can look back at the Biden administration and conclude that the backbone America, and the world, needed in American leadership, was adequate. Former President Biden's decorum was leagues above his predecessor, and he was a genuine and well-meaning president – even if misguided at times – but there was something pervasive to his administration that made attuned observers conclude that they would fold if they were taken to task or things got too tough.

But don't take my word for it – the Taliban called their bluff in 2021 in Afghanistan, Putin called it in 2022 in Ukraine, Hamas and Iran called it in 2023 in Israel, and even the Democratic Party, and ultimately the American people, called it in 2024.

Individual presidents aside, the point here is that *toughness* in American leadership matters, but a projection, nor a veil of toughness, will suffice. It must be *real* to the core.

So. Is America tough to its core? It has become a hobby for our adversaries and even American media (depending on the outlet, and which party has the presidency) to obsess over why America is weak, declining, and on its last leg.

But, let me share with you why America is, in fact, tough.

## American Power

If you ever want to get a taste for the significance of *power* in human nature, try this experiment. Tell your significant other or close friend you need to talk, sit them down, and ask one "simple" question: who has the *power* in our relationship?

Things are going to get peanut-butter-and-mustard-awkward for you, real quick. So, on second thought, definitely do not do this – just leave it as a thought exercise. Yet, notice that feeling we all felt there. This is why *power* is a topic as old and foundational as life itself.

There are many ways to think about power. However, when it comes to nations there is a tidy acronym to assist us: *DIIME*. This concept is often used by the U.S. military, albeit with one 'I.' I've added a second 'I' to capture a concept that I see as the source of all the other elements of national power.

*DIIME*, with two I's, stands for: *Diplomacy, Information, Institutions, Military, and Economy*.

With that said, let's discuss what America brings to the table when it comes to national power. I'll begin with my addition to the standard acronym – Institutions – and continue in order (as I see it) up the escalatory chain of national power with Information, Diplomacy, Economy, and lastly, the most obvious form of power, the Military.

## Institutions

As the source of all the other elements of power, institutions tend to be foundational concepts for a nation. For this reason, I use a broad definition of the term for the purposes of DIIME power.

There are many American institutions, but just to name a few: our system of constitutional democracy, a culture of individual liberty and the protection of equal rights, a culture of freedom of speech and religion, private property rights including intellectual property, the rule of law, a competitive market-driven economy, a culture of leading-edge technology development (e.g., in natural resources, Silicon Valley tech, and beyond), many strong social institutions (e.g., education, family, and more), and lastly, what I call *population dynamism*, which has been built over centuries by attracting the brave and ambitious peoples of the world to America.

These institutions took time to build and solidify, and as such, are the bedrock of America. Yet, they are not immune from pressure, fracturing, and even total erosion.

This is why as a nation, above all else, we must prize our institutions as the phenomenon that they are in their totality. We should be vigilant in our recognition of pressure on our institutions; fearless in challenging destroyers, and courageous in our willingness to reform them when decay creeps in; and ultimately, we should be relentless in our efforts to preserve them.

**Information**

The idea that "information is power" is one that all Americans can identify with. So, what does this look like for a nation?

American information as an arm of national power can be thought of in two categories: direct and indirect. The direct side of things is more straightforward to grasp (even if something is done in secret from the general public, at times). These are things such as internet, television, and radio broadcasts, military information, and intelligence operations (e.g., CIA).

While on the indirect side of things, or more difficult to grasp at times, are things such as general Americana brand power, American music, movies, and sports, and even American companies (e.g., from Coca-Cola to NASA). These are a few examples, but there is much, much more that could be listed.

Impacting hearts and minds is power, and when this is done by an entity or idea associated with the U.S., this is American power at work. This is often a *softer* form of power, or in other words, it is not always obvious it's being used and it can take time to have an impact. Yet, it would be a mistake to conclude it is any less powerful than something more direct, like say, bombing another country with a *huuuge*, gold-plated missile.

For many decades, America has been second to none when it comes to information power, both in our government and private sector capabilities. But, we must continue to invest in, and bring awareness to, the value of these capabilities in providing for our nation's *long-term* security and prosperity.

**Diplomacy**

In its simplest conception, diplomacy is merely discussions and negotiations between nations. All nations have some level of diplomatic power. And on its face, America's specific diplomatic power may not look especially unique. However, once again, for many decades America has had an outsized ability to impact nation-to-nation and multilateral discussions.

This includes the U.S.' primary role in setting up multilateral organizations after the chaos of

World War II, such as the United Nations (UN); it includes the ability to establish large trade agreements and single-handedly impact the global flow of goods and services (for better and for worse); and, it includes America's unique ability to broker ceasefire agreements and establish dozens of military partnerships and formal alliances, such as the recently revitalized and formidable North Atlantic Treaty Organization (NATO).

Further, as is the case with the U.S., a high level of diplomatic power is typically underpinned by significant economic and/or military power. And, although it is certainly a hand that can be overplayed or rendered useless in extreme scenarios, diplomacy is an element of national power that is inherently peaceful and should be among the first choices for all nations, including America.

## Economy

The power of the American economy is no secret. However, until recently, and likely still not in full, many people did not realize how deeply American power is embedded in the global economic system. Although this power has continued to grow since the nation's early days, it should not surprise you at this point that this was another trend that escalated sharply at the conclusion of World War II.

America's economic power includes, for one, the sheer size of the American economy as the largest in the world at ~25% of global GDP or economic activity. For comparison, in second place is China's economy at ~15%, and next is Germany at a distant third with ~4%.

Another attribute of American economic power includes the widespread use of the American financial system and the dollar, including as the world's reserve currency (or in other words, nations want to hold U.S. dollars in their central banks more than any other currency in the world).

Further, the economic power of America includes the economic aid and financial influence provided by U.S.-led organizations such as the International Monetary Fund (IMF) and World Bank; and lastly, although there is much more that could be listed, our economic power includes America's renowned entrepreneurial culture and innovative capacity, from small businesses that are blanketed across the country to U.S. multinational corporate powerhouses, including 17 of the 20 most valuable companies in the world.

Everyday Americans should remain well aware that all of this economic power provides America with tremendous advantages, above and beyond Americans' pocketbooks.

**Military**

'The United States military' is four words that make shit happen.

There is a lot that is known, and unknown ("that's classified"), about the American military, but most fully appreciate just how dominant it is. Of course, other nations, particularly our adversaries, will dispute this on the margins, but overall it is clear that the U.S. military is the most advanced, well-funded, and feared military in the world.

The following are *just a few* attributes of American military power that even everyday Americans may not be familiar with: the U.S. military has a global force and command structure that spans every ocean, continent, and even space above, including over 750 overseas military bases in over 80 countries (for comparison, most countries have none or a few, with the UK and Russia potentially having a few dozen, but estimates vary widely); further, the U.S. has military personnel in over 150 countries across the world; American veterans and service members are a battle-hardened, experienced force (an unfortunate reality, but also an advantage once earned); and lastly, supporting the U.S. military is an increasingly innovative and entrepreneurial defense industrial base, not limited to 5 of the 6 largest defense companies in the world.

The U.S. military is formidable, and our service members are the most capable and professional in the world. This should be a source of pride for all Americans, and we should be reverent of the sacrifices that have been made.

The military is an element of national power that backstops all other forms of power, or in other words, it is who we look to as a nation when all else fails.

Using military force is not a decision Americans should ever take lightly, but when we do, we can do so with the confidence that we are sending the best in the world.

And so, I ask again, is America tough to its core? I trust that your answer, like mine, is an unequivocal, "yes."

America's adversaries will see U.S. presidents come and go, they will see Americans argue publicly as democracies do, and they will see our political parties fight like rabid dogs – and ultimately, they may think the end is near for us.

However, when it comes to *Principle #3*, they should know this: no matter our disagreements, no matter which president is in office, and no matter the political drama of the moment – the American people's *toughness* runs deep, it is *resilient*, and it *will* endure.

Or, as Teddy would say: America carries a big stick.

# The New Order

In conclusion, as a nation, how does America win *The Great Disorder* we now find ourselves in?

We begin by dispassionately discussing and evaluating the state of our current condition. We then must be honest about the disruption that was sorely needed, and persist in its execution, while courageously speaking truth to power when bad decisions are made and unnecessary chaos created. This requires everyday Americans, and our leaders, to strongly reject *The New Rules* and enthusiastically embrace the three *Principles* discussed in this book.

To do so is a winning strategy for America, and as the indispensable leader of the free world, a winning strategy for global stability and prosperity.

The Great Disorder

# *Appendix*

# Discovering America's North Star

Question for you. Does America live by its *values* or its *interests*? What about you, personally?

As I've discussed before, at the highest level, America's primary objective in world affairs should be to *Lead with American Values & Defend American Interests*. However, what *are* our values, what are our interests, and are they always aligned?

Consider a few quotes from U.S. presidents:

- "The *interests* of a nation, when well understood, will be found to coincide with their moral duties." (Thomas Jefferson (author) for George Washington (orator), 1792)

- "Our American *values* are not luxuries, but necessities -- not the salt in our bread, but the bread itself." (Jimmy Carter, 1981)

- "Our families nurture, preserve, and pass on to each succeeding generation the *values* we share and cherish, *values* that are the foundation of our freedoms." (Ronald Reagan, 1985)

- "When our *interests* and *values* are at stake, we have a responsibility to act." (Barack Obama, 2011)

- "I'm here today to represent the *interests* of the American people and to affirm America's friendship and partnership in building a better world." (Donald Trump, 2018)

There's clearly something fundamentally important about American values and interests. What is not clear is what is actually meant when these words are used – even by our leaders in the highest office.

Yet, understanding their meaning is not merely an academic exercise, it's essential to establishing a *common language* between leaders and citizens. Without it, "the People" are flying blind.

Let's start with values. In a previous discussion, I laid out a simple framework for thinking about American values. I dubbed it *The American Values Meal* – a topic all Americans can identify with, because let's be honest, what's more Americana than fast cars and fast food? As cheesy as it may seem (sorry, if we're talkin' buns, I'm talkin' puns), *The American Values Meal* gets to the heart of American values.

A thorough dissection can always provide more detail, but let's lay out the important elements to remember.

## The American Values Meal

**Order**. You're cruising down the road, your stomach growls like a rabid dog, and a glorious sign emerges in the distance – one you know oh so well. As you skid into your favorite fast-food joint on two wheels, there's one thing you have to do first before your taste buds reach the promised land ...*Order*.

For nations, without *Order*, no other values can be secured. A nation that doesn't establish *order and the rule of law* from the beginning – both in its constitution and in its culture – will not be a nation for long. Not surprisingly, it is no coincidence that a significant number of America's Founding Fathers and even members of Congress today have backgrounds in law.

**Democracy**. When you pull up to the window, and that bag of deliciousness is handed to you, at its *core* is your entrée. Quite likely, it's a burger – since this is America and no food screams stars and stripes like a good burger – but more specifically, we're going to call it a *Democracy Burger*.

In any democratic form of government, such as in a republic as we have in the U.S., the government derives its power from the people. It does not seize power through force or inherit it from a bloodline. Power is granted, temporarily, through elections by "the People." This ideal is *core* to American values.

**Freedom**. Even though that burger's on your mind, I'll bet two shakes of salt that when your hand nosedives into the bag, the first thing you're pulling out is a few fries. I'll also bet that you would savor them even more if you knew they were *Freedom Fries*.

In America, we cherish individual liberty and free people, freedom of speech, freedom of religion, the list goes on. *Freedom...* is the word on the tip of the tongue of every American. It's just who we are.

**Fairness**. Maybe you made it home, or maybe you pulled the e-brake after spotting the first empty parking spot coming out of the drive thru. Either way, after a few bites of your burger and fries, you're washing it down with something. I contend, that a shake is the way to go, and it tastes even better if it's a *Fair Shake.*

Call it what you will – a fair shake, an equal opportunity, etc. – no matter your background, title, or riches, America is built upon the ideal that every person gets their shot.

**Rights**. You've finished your meal, your euphoria has reached its cruising altitude, and all is right in the world. But it's at this moment that you realize the bag's not empty. The cashier must have noticed that childlike twinkle in your eye and inconspicuously slipped a bundle of joy into the bottom of the bag. Yes.. it's a toy. But not just any toy – *The Rights Toy.*

Just like the toy in a kid's meal is all but a birthright in America, so too are Americans' rights. Americans are not just free, we have "unalienable rights" enshrined explicitly and forever in our Constitution and the Bill of Rights.

Order, Democracy Burger, Freedom Fries, a Fair Shake, and The Rights Toy – that is *The American Values Meal. These* are our values, and together they are unabashedly American, made in the USA and served worldwide.

## American Interests

So that's American values, but what about interests?

Tabling the food metaphors for now, interests, as important as they are to a nation, are actually fairly simple to explain.

Although the phrase is often used ambiguously and as a catchall justification for any and all government decisions, American interests fundamentally boil down to two things: national security and prosperity.

National security can most simply be thought of as the physical safety and security of Americans, while prosperity as Americans' economic security and future potential. That's the crux of it.

## Making a Choice

Now that we have a common understanding of American values and interests, let's return to the questions I posed at the beginning. Does America live by its values or its interests? What about you, personally?

In a perfect world, it's both, and American values and interests are always aligned. Although we should aspire for alignment, in the real world, this is not possible for every decision and we must choose which to prioritize.

I understand this reality may be difficult for our more idealist tendencies to come to terms with. Certainly, in our personal lives, we all have red lines that we do not cross, and most of us seek to prevent compromising on our values.

In most cases, this is achievable with a principled foundation and a dash of discipline. Yet, it's not too difficult to imagine a scenario in which the most challenging of moral dilemmas can arise.

Step into the gray with me for a moment. Imagine your family is starving and nearing death. What food that's available in the community is scarce, but you have none. Would you *steal* to feed them? …Would you *kill* to feed them?

Let's broaden the impact of your decision to another wickedly difficult, albeit hypothetical scenario – you've been given the power to go back in time to the moment of Hitler's birth. You're alone with him, next to his crib, in the dead of night. Would you *kill* him, an infant?

If taken seriously, these are clearly not easy questions to answer. The mental gymnastics we all do to explain our decisions in these scenarios is the essence of moral philosophy.

Now. Expand moral dilemmas like these to a nation with hundreds of millions of people and the most significant global role in history. Whether we're always aware of it or not, at any given moment, hundreds if not thousands of extremely difficult decisions are being made by our elected leadership, military, intelligence services, and more, at home and across the world. And as already mentioned, their power is ultimately derived from "the People."

So, with that said, what should be their – and by extension, our – *north star* when making these decisions?

Making the 'right' choice time and time again is no small feat. Hindsight is 20/20 and it's easy for some to look in the rearview mirror of history and judge specific decisions as 'bad'. No doubt some were, because let's be honest, we've done some dumb shit. Yet, even with our fair share of scars and bad actors, I do believe the *foundation* of America is fundamentally good and our combined ideals exceptional.

That is why my position is that our *north star* should be to *Lead with American Values & Defend American Interests*.

Moreover, staying clear-eyed about the world as it is and not as we wish it to be, we must prioritize securing our core interests. We should do this while living out our values to the best of our ability, but an America without its core interests secured will not be an America at all – and American values will become all but irrelevant.

When our core interests are secured, not only is it easier to lead with our values, we then have opportunities to promote them throughout the world – keeping in mind that this is a means to a goal, not the goal itself. As, a world safer for American values is a world safer for American interests, vice versa, and on and on the flywheel spins.

In sum, here is how I see it. Both values and interests are fundamental to the decisions that we make, but they require different considerations. Values are how we think the world *should be*; they are principled and idealist in nature. Interests are how the world is *in reality;* they are practical and realist in nature.

It's fantastic when neither needs to be sacrificed for the sake of the other, which can be the case for many of our daily decisions. However, in those inevitable dilemmas, how do *we* make our decisions? How do *you* make your decisions? What is our *north star*?

What we decide in these moments can be incredibly revealing of who we are at our core, and over time, will come to define us.

Thomas Jefferson knew this over 200 years ago, and 200 years from now, these ideals will continue to ring true.

# The Great Disorder

# Afterword

I began writing *The Great Disorder* around the second Trump administration's first 100 days in office, in April 2025, once it became clearer what their general approach to governing and international relations would be.

Some moves were predictable, while others surprised even President Trump's political base. Regardless, most media reporting continued the approach of characterizing every move the President made as amazing or horrendous –

there was no in between. It was an extreme version of humanity's most basic instinct: tribalism. Everything was, obviously, right or wrong, good or evil, black or white.

Yet, what about the many shades of gray? *Navigating the gray* in life is when we learn, when we grow, and when we are pressure tested before we make the most important decisions of our lives – the decisions that form our character, impact our families' well-being, and chart the course of our livelihoods and our nation.

And so, this was the story I knew I had to tell: how to navigate the gray during *The Great Disorder* and not only come out alive on the other side, but come out thriving in a new, principled world order.

There is no single answer for Americans to look to in order to achieve this, and certainly no arbitrary *New Rules* that should guide us. What we do have are our core interests and American values (i.e., our north star) that we can consult to create *Principles* to guide our leaders and the nation. And with these in hand, we have the bones of a winning strategy for America.

After developing these to be fit for the moment, I began to write *The Great Disorder: An American Manifesto for a New World Order*. My writing progressed from a short essay shared with family and friends, to a much longer essay, to eventually, this short book.

By reading it, my goals are that: you now recognize the gray in situations that previously appeared only to be black or white; you are better equipped to navigate this terrain amidst the chaos of our current geopolitical environment; and, you see America's challenges, not with despair, but with realistic optimism and as an opportunity to create solutions for a more prosperous future.

If that message resonates with you, my hope is that you will spread it and use it to make a positive impact in your sphere of influence. Moreover, in addition to sharing this book with family, friends, and colleagues, I also want to invite you to join the movement that continues the work we have discussed here.

At my company – Dear America Network – our mission is to make sense of America's relationship with the world. Moreover, if you believe in American values and our leadership role, are curious about how the world works, are a fearless truth seeker, and a relentless problem solver – join us.

Visit our website to learn more and to connect directly about contributing to our movement.

# Afterword

We have only just begun.


Think freely,


Zack Spratling

Founder & CEO

Dear America Network

October 2025

# The Great Disorder

# An American Manifesto for a New World Order

Dear America
NETWORK

DearAmericaNetwork.com

Printed in Dunstable, United Kingdom